T0288402

Get Home!

CONTENTS

NATIONAL GEOGRAPHIC School Publishing
Hampton-Brown

e

Words with Short e

Look at each picture. Read the words.

Example:

b**e**d

w**e**b

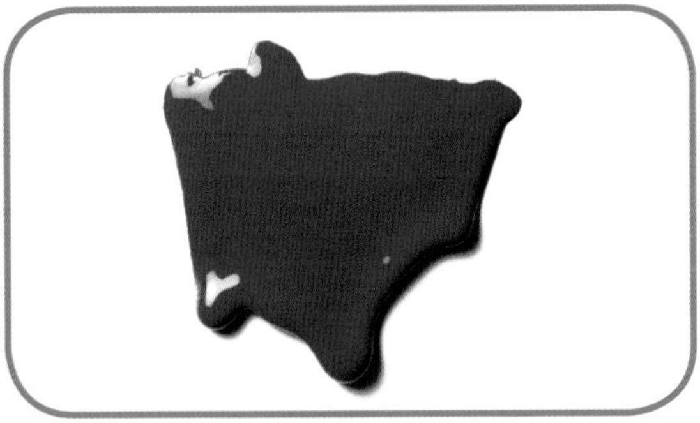

r**e**d

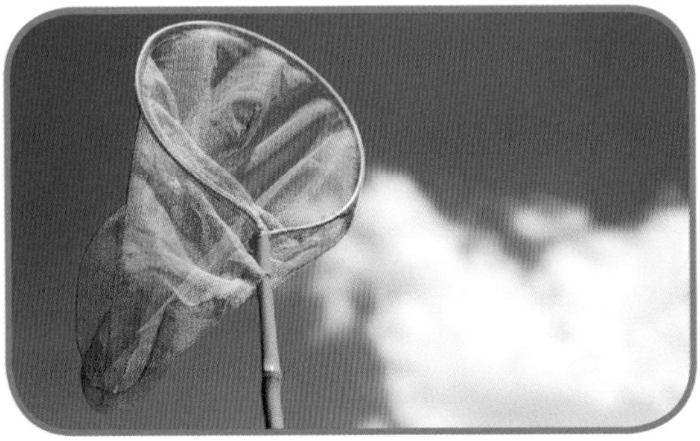

n**e**t

High Frequency **Words**

be
down
or
their
them
they
with
your

Key Words

Look at the picture. Read the sentences.

The Pet Shop

1. Look up **or** look **down** and you will see pets.
2. People like **their** pets.
3. **They** can have fun **with them**.
4. Will you get a pet?
5. Will **your** pet **be** a dog or a cat?

Phonics Games

NGReach.com

Big City, Little Town

by Suzy Shaffer

A big city is a hectic spot.

It has a lot of people on the go. Look up and down. You can see a lot of people. They fit in a little space.

A big city has a lot of traffic.

Vans zip up and down. Cabs zigzag in and out.

Yet, a big city can be like a little town.

This neighborhood is like a little town in a big city. It has shops and a market.

People can get pretzels from a stand.
They can get a trim from the barber.

Your pet can get help from the vet.

Kids can see their pals at the bike shop.

Moms and dads can visit with their pals, too!

A neighborhood is like a little town hidden in the center of a big city.

Words with Short e

Read these words.

bed	ten	pet	net
get	set	bad	wet

Find the words with short **e**.
Use letters to build them.

g e t

Talk Together

Choose words from the box above to to tell what the man can get at the shops.

The man can get a pet.

u

Words with Short u

Look at each picture. Read the words.

Example:

cup

sun

hut

bus

run

rug

High Frequency Words
be
down
or
their
them
they
with
your

Key Words

Look at the picture. Read the sentences.

Have Fun!

1. Have fun **with** **your** pals.
2. What do **they** like to do? Ask **them**.
3. They can run **down** a hill **or** go for a ride.
4. They can go with **their** pets!
5. It will **be** fun.

Phonics Games

NGReach.com

Homes

by Alejo Balingit

What is a home? A home is a place for you!

A home can be in a little town or in a big city. It can be in a neighborhood or be by itself on a big plot of land.

Some kids have homes in huts.
This is a mud hut.

A lot of huts in one place are like a little town.

Some kids have homes in big city apartments. They can get on a bus to go from place to place.

There are lots of traffic jams and lots of people in a big city.

Some kids do not have homes in a town or in a big city. They are far from their pals.

They can not get on a bus to go
to see them. They must get a ride.

Look at all the homes!

Are all homes the same? Not at all!

No matter what it is like, there is no place like home! ❖

Words with Short u

Read these words.

nut	rug	mud	cat	hut
cup	tip	bus	fun	man

Find the words with short **u**.
Use letters to build them.

n u t

Talk Together

Choose words from the box above to tell your partner about the picture.

The bus is in the mud.

Where Is Edwin?

Look at the picture with a partner. Take turns reading the clues. Then find Edwin.

1. Edwin has a red hat.
2. He is with his pet.
3. They are by a hut.
4. Their hut is tan or red.
5. Their hut has a cactus.
6. Their hut has a flag, but it is hidden.

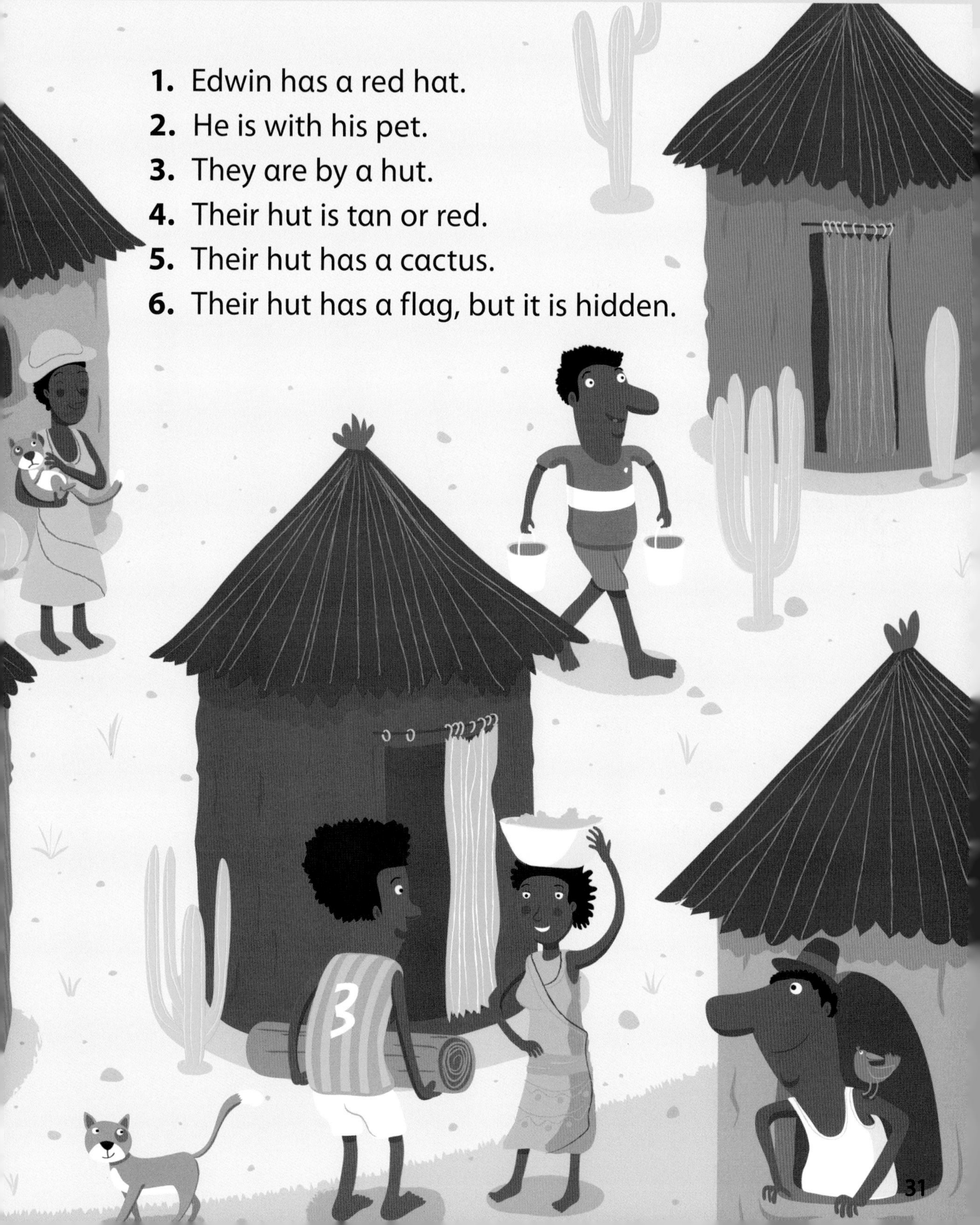

Acknowledgments
Grateful acknowledgment is given to the authors, artists, photographers, museums, publishers, and agents for permission to reprint copyrighted material. Every effort has been made to secure the appropriate permission. If any omissions have been made or if corrections are required, please contact the Publisher.

Photographic Credits
CVR g bell/Alamy Images. **2** (bl) Ivonne Wierink/Shutterstock. (br) Mark Hatfield/iStockphoto. (cl) Picsfive/Shutterstock. (cr) dzianis miraniuk/iStockphoto. (tl) Galayko Sergey/Shutterstock. **3** Liz Garza Williams/Hampton-Brown/National Geographic School Publishing. **4-5** Chad Ehlers/Alamy Images. **6-7** (l) Jodi Cobb/National Geographic Image Collection. **7** (inset) DNY59/iStockphoto. **8-9** (l) Panoramic Images/Getty Images. **9** (bg) Suto Norbert Zsolt/Shutterstock. (inset) Robin MacDougall/Getty Images. **10** (b) Daniel Bosler/Getty Images. (t) Oberhaeuser/Caro/Alamy Images. **10-11** (bg) Suto Norbert Zsolt/Shutterstock. **11** (inset) LWA-Dann Tardif/Corbis. **12** (bg) Suto Norbert Zsolt/Shutterstock. (inset) Michael Newman/PhotoEdit. **12-13** (r) MoMo Productions/Getty Images. **14** (bg) Suto Norbert Zsolt/Shutterstock. (inset) Manfred Gottschalk/age fotostock. **15** Liz Garza Williams/Hampton-Brown/National Geographic School Publishing. **16** (bl) Jacek Chabraszewski/Shutterstock. (br) Helle Bro/iStockphoto. (brc) Robert Madeira/Shutterstock. (cl) Vishal Shah/Shutterstock. (tl) Artem Povarov/iStockphoto. (trc) Jakubski/Shutterstock. **17** Liz Garza Williams/Hampton-Brown/National Geographic School Publishing. **18** (l) Christian Delbert/Shutterstock. (r) Ken Cave/Shutterstock. **19** (l) ligonography/iStockphoto. (r) Angel Herrero de Frutos/iStockphoto. **20-21** (l) Jodi Cobb/National Geographic Image Collection. **21** Thomas J. Abercrombie/National Geographic Image Collection. **22** Lee Snider/The Image Works, Inc. **23-24** (r) Mark Henley/age fotostock. **24-25** (l) Barrett & MacKay/All Canada Photos/Photolibrary. **25** Stephen Stickler/Getty Images. **26** (bl, tl) Elena Elisseeva/Shutterstock. **26-27** (bc) Mark Karrass/Corbis Premium RF/Alamy Images. (tc) Mikhail Nekrasov/Shutterstock. **27** (br) andydidyk/iStockphoto. (tr) Diana Lundin/Shutterstock. **28** David Sacks/Getty Images. **29** Liz Garza Williams/Hampton-Brown/National Geographic School Publishing.

Illustrator Credits
3, 15, 17, 29 Peter Grosshauer; **30-31** Mattia Cerato

National Geographic School Publishing
Hampton-Brown
www.NGSP.com

Printed in the USA.
Quad Graphics, Leominster, MA

ISBN:978-0-7362-8058-7

18 19
10 9 8 7